ETHEL
AND THE
POTS

Maite Butron & Brady Ough
Illustrated by Rafael Butron

Ethel Publications
Australia
Copyright © 2018 by Maite Butron & Brady Ough
Illustrations Copyright © 2018 by Rafael Butron

Written by
Maite Butron & Brady Ough

Illustrated by Rafael Butron

Edited by Morgana Willing

ISBN 978-0-6483126-0-4
ISBN 978-0-6483126-1-1 (ebook)

... INTRODUCTION

The Ethel the Echidna series are childrens' books with simple stories that gently highlight boundaries, both internal and external for the healthy growth of young human beings.

These stories also introduce the practice of mindfulness, emphasizing the importance of awareness about choice when it comes to behaviour.

The stories are accompanied by beautiful drawings that capture Ethel and her friends' everyday lives, laughter and organic feelings and they will simply capture your heart.

ETHEL
AND THE
POTS

... A PARENTS' GUIDE

This story was designed to address the concepts of boundaries and emotional regulation.

Boundaries are defined as set limits or filters that guide appropriate, ethical and respectful behaviour.

In this story, Jeremy displays effective boundaries by refusing to give away something that does not belong to him.

Ethel displays effective emotional regulation. She does this by recognising her feelings and accepting them. She uses a mindful tool – breathing – to centre herself. This allows her to continue her interaction with Jeremy without unhelpful arguments.

Due to Ethel and Jeremy's choices, they both avoid unnecessary conflict.

Ethel the echidna loved
her friends and family.

Usually, everyone got
on very well… until one
Wednesday afternoon when
everything went a little dotty
and a tiny bit potty.

It all started when Ethel went to her best friend Jeremy's house and saw his beautiful potted plants.

Jeremy had clay pots with interesting carvings and paintings on the outside. Inside the pots were differently coloured flowers.

Ethel was very impressed with the way the potted plants looked and felt inspired to make her own lovely garden.

Ethel became very excited by this idea and imagined that her potted plants would look even nicer than Jeremy's. Her flowers would be brighter and her clay pots would look even more special.

While imagining what her garden would look like, Ethel saw some empty clay pots to the side of Jeremy's garden.

"Jeremy, can I please borrow that empty clay pot with the green and yellow spots?" Ethel asked politely.

"I'm sorry Ethel,"
responded Jeremy calmly,
"I can't lend you that pot."

Ethel felt her face become hot.

"You can't lend it to me?" she asked, a little too loudly.

All Ethel could think was that Jeremy was trying to ruin the garden she had been imagining on purpose.

Ethel decided she was never going to speak to Jeremy again. She wasn't going to make him any more dinners and she wasn't going to give him any more presents.

Ethel's hands had become fists and she felt as though steam might start coming out of her ears.

Ethel was about to start yelling at Jeremy, but she suddenly remembered that Granny M had told her to take ten deep breaths when she felt angry.

Slowly, Ethel took ten deep breaths.

Surprisingly, Ethel started to feel better. She didn't feel as angry with Jeremy anymore, and she no longer wanted to yell at him.

Instead, using a voice that was only a tiny bit shaky Ethel asked, *"Jeremy, why won't you lend me your pot? Don't you want me to have a beautiful garden as well?"*

Calmly, Jeremy replied,
*"Oh Ethel, of course I want
you to have a beautiful
garden too, I just can't lend
you the pot with the green
and yellow spots because it
belongs to Clive."*

Jeremy pointed to three lovely pots leaning against a mossy boulder and said, *"those pots belong to me, you can borrow one if you like Ethel"*.

Ethel was very relieved that she hadn't yelled at Jeremy over something so small and happily chose a pot with red polka dots to borrow.

Now that Ethel had a pot to use in her garden thanks to Jeremy, she invited him over to celebrate by eating a large plateful of crispy ants washed down with a cup of pumpkin and spider juice.

Pumpkin and Spider Juice

Ingredients:
1 Pumpkin
2 Cups assorted spiders
15 Spider webs (include all bugs caught in webs)
4 Cups chilled rainwater

1. Cut up pumpkin and place on oven tray. Include pumpkin skin and seeds.
2. Place tray in the oven for the time it takes to watch a full episode of "All Echidnas Great and Small".
3. Place pumpkin, spiders and webs into a stone bowl and smash, crash and bash until ingredients have made a smooth pulp.
4. Add water and stir thoroughly.
5. Pour into your favourite highballs and serve chilled.

For Echidnas Only

Crispy Ants

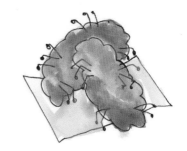

Making crispy ants is a very important part of the Echidna community. This is because for the recipe to work best, everyone needs to help.

The secret to delicious crispy ants is variety. Use different types of ants - all colours and sizes from as many varied nests as possible. All Echidnas' have their own special (and often hidden) ant hunting spots.

1. Each Echidna should put two cups of their favourite ants into a mixing bowl.
2. When four buckets of ants have been collected, spread the ants out on a large flat rock in the sun.
3. Construct a covering made from mosquito netting or muslin and sticks and place this approximately thirty centimetres over the ants.
4. Roasting must take place over seven days and seven nights.
5. Make sure at least two Echidnas are keeping guard at all times to ensure no one is tempted into eating the ants early.
6. If it begins to rain, cover the netting with large leaves to keep the ants dry.
7. When the ants are thoroughly crispy, carefully sweep all ants off the rock and evenly divide them into portions for all community members.

Crispy ants are the ultimate trail mix for Echidnas, and a great example of a community working together.

For Echidnas Only

This story was written by Brady Ough.
He is a parent, grandparent, chef, massage
therapist and energetic healer.

Concept and parenting guide by Maite Butron.
She is a parent and grandparent who works as
a Holistic Counsellor, Relationship Counsellor
and Life Coach.

Both authors are passionate about boundaries
and active, respectful parenting.

Original watercolour drawings by
Rafael Butron, artist and parent.

Edited by Morgana Willing, parent and
early childhood educator.

Recipe inspirations and fun add-ons by
Sofia Hartley.

Design by Vicente Butron, artist, BA&D.

Eternal gratitude to Ben Jarvis, for
his intellectual and legal guidance.

Printed in Great Britain
by Amazon

31966268R00027